The Official
Manchester City
Annual 2009

Written by David Clayton

A Grange Publication

© 2008. Published by Grange Communications Ltd., Edinburgh under licence from Manchester City Football Club. Printed in the EU.

Photographs © PA Photos & MCFC
ISBN 978 1 906211 38 7

£6.99

Contents

Welcome to the official Manchester City Annual 2009! Packed with quizzes, profiles, stats and posters, we hope you find this year's annual the best ever and with such an exciting season ahead, this could be an unforgettable year in the history of the Blues.

We kick off with a few words from our new manager, Mark Hughes, who will be hoping to bring back a trophy or two to the City of Manchester Stadium over the next few years.

Then we move on to the Season Report where we look at what went right – and wrong – during last year's dramatic campaign.

City are back in Europe and to celebrate, we look at the Blues' complete history in all European competitions.

There are profiles on some of the club's most popular players such as Joe Hart, Micah Richards, Martin Petrov and Michael Johnson, as well as a look at the new players that have arrived over the summer.

There is a focus on the Academy plus the players to look out for in 2009 – all this plus loads of quizzes and puzzles to keep you busy. Have fun!

David Clayton, Editor

Hughes the Man!

Meet City's new manager - Mark Hughes

City wasted little time in identifying the man they wanted to succeed Sven-Goran Eriksson at the end of last season and within days of the position being vacated Mark Hughes was installed as the new manager of Manchester City.

Hughes is one of the most well respected young managers in England and despite being linked with a number of other top jobs in the past couple of years, when City registered their official interest, he was only too happy to accept. Born in Wrexham, Hughes joined Manchester United as a teenager and spent six years at Old Trafford before joining Barcelona in 1986. He was then loaned out to Bayern Munich for a season before returning to Manchester United for a further seven-year spell where he became something of a legend as well as representing Wales with great distinction, winning 72 caps over a 15-year period. Despite being 32, he was still one of the most sought-after strikers in the country, Chelsea signed him in 1995 and he became a huge favourite at Stamford Bridge during the three years he spent there.

Aged 35, the evergreen Hughes – nicknamed 'Sparky' – wasn't quite ready to hang his boots up and he then signed for Southampton in 1998, playing more of a midfield role, before moving on again, this time to Everton. While at Goodison Park, he became manager of Wales and almost steered his country to Euro 2004 – an incredible achievement considering the state of Welsh football when he took over. He finished his playing career with Blackburn Rovers, officially retiring as a player in 2002.

He left his post as Wales boss in September 2004 to become manager of Blackburn and managed to keep the Ewood

Everyone knows how loyal City fans are and what magnificent support they give and I am looking forward to managing a successful side in a full stadium

Park side in the Premier League after they had seemed set for relegation. He also guided them to their first FA Cup semi-final for 40 years!

Hughes then inspired Rovers to a top-six finish in his first full season, making them an attractive and difficult side to play against in the process. His astuteness in the transfer market saw him bring in the likes of Benni McCarthy, Christopher Samba, Roque Santa Cruz, David Bentley, Ryan Nelsen and Neil Warnock for a combined fee of less than £9m – and all are now worth considerably more than Hughes paid for them.

He also took Rovers to the League Cup semi-final and another FA Cup semi-final, as well as finishing in the top ten in 2007/08 for a third successive season – no wonder the Blues wanted him to be the new manager.

Of the future, Hughes said: "City fans have always impressed me, I have lived in the area now since 1988 and I am aware of the passion and love for their club that City fans have. My message to them is that I am delighted to be here.

"They have already given me great support and I have been pleased with the positive reaction. They know my teams work hard and are committed and I can tell them that we will play attacking technical football.

"Everyone knows how loyal City fans are and what magnificent support they give and I am looking forward to managing a successful side in a full stadium.

"It didn't take any time for me to make my mind up that City was the right place. I enjoyed my time at Blackburn but there was a limit to where we could go. I needed to move to a club that matched my ambitions and I have. I am really excited."

2007/2008 Season Review

The Story of the 2007/08 Season

August

With seven new signings, a new manager, a new owner and a new kit, City were unrecognisable as they ran out to face West Ham United on the opening day of the 2007/08 campaign. Backed by 4,000 travelling fans, the Blues handed debuts to Kasper Schmeichel, Vedran Corluka, Javier Garrido, Elano, Martin Petrov and Rolando Bianchi, with Valeri Bojinov and Geovanni on the subs' bench.
Sven-Goran Eriksson had only been in charge for six weeks, but his side played as though they'd known each other for years and goals from Bianchi and Geovanni gave the Swede – and new owner and Chairman Dr Thaksin Shinawatra – a dream start as they brushed aside the Hammers 2-0.
Four days later, Derby County arrived at the City of Manchester Stadium. Though the Rams were already red-hot favourites for relegation, they more than matched the Blues on the night and only a wonderful goal from Michael Johnson separated the two teams.

City then went into the Manchester derby knowing a win would put them top of the table, but the loss of Bojinov for the entire season after just a few minutes cast a shadow on the match, which Manchester United began to dominate – but neat work from Elano found Geovanni in space 25 yards from goal and the Brazilian unleashed a powerful shot that deflected slightly off Vidic to beat Edwin van der Sar and give the Blues a 1-0 win. The fans were loving it and Sven and his team couldn't have imagined things would have begun so well – but next up was a severe test of his new team's ability – away to Arsenal.
The Blues seemed to be heading for a well-earned point – especially after Schmeichel saved a Robin van Persie penalty, but the hosts scored a late winner to spoil an otherwise perfect August, which ended with a 2-1 Carling Cup win at Bristol City with goals from Bianchi and Emile Mpenza.

P 5 W 4 D 0 L 1 F 6 A 2

September

September proved to be another exciting month for the new-look Blues, despite starting with a narrow 1-0 defeat to Blackburn Rovers. City returned from a two-week international break with an impressive 1-0 home win over Aston Villa thanks to Michael Johnson's superb individual goal and a week later, City were involved in an entertaining 3-3 draw at Fulham, Martin Petrov scoring his first two goals for the club and Mpenza adding the other. A last-minute winner from Georgios Samaras edged City into the last 16 of the Carling Cup with a hard-fought 1-0 win over Norwich City, but it was the next league game that caused the rest of the Premier League to sit up and take the Blues seriously as Eriksson's side turned on the style in a magnificent 3-1 home win over Newcastle. The football was sparkling and goals from Petrov, Mpenza and a wonder free-kick from Elano sent the fans home in ecstasy.

P 5 W 3 D 1 L 1 F 8 A 5

October

A mixed month for City who maintained their 100% home record but also suffered a record Premier League defeat, too. Elano scored a superb brace against Middlesbrough and Bianchi added another as City won 3-1 against Middlesbrough and two weeks later Elano's first-half strike against Birmingham made it an incredible six home wins in a row to keep the Blues in the Champions League places. But with the chance of proving the challenge for the title was no fluke, Eriksson's side turned in a nightmare performance that Chelsea took full advantage of – City lost 6-0. However they gained a 1-0 Carling Cup win at Bolton. But the question marks still remained after the Stamford Bridge nightmare…

P 4 W 3 D 0 L 1 F 5 A 7

2007/2008 Season Review

The Story of the 2007/08 Season

November

Stephen Ireland's goal was enough to see a spirited Sunderland off at the City of Manchester Stadium as the Blues made it a magnificent seven straight home victories and after a respectable 0-0 draw at Portsmouth, Ireland was again the hero as his injury time volley against Reading made it eight. City were in the top four on merit and the 6-0 defeat at Chelsea was now considered to be nothing more than a blip.

P 3 W 2 D 1 L 0 F 3 A 1

December

With six league games and a Carling Cup quarter-final to play, December was always going to be a make-or-break month for City. If they were still in the top four going into the New Year, who knew how high they could go? A first-minute goal from Geovanni at Wigan was the perfect start to the month, but the Latics fought back to draw 1-1. A 2-1 defeat at Spurs followed, but City's home form came to the rescue when, despite falling 2-1 behind to Bolton, the Blues ran out 4-2 winners to make it nine home wins on the bounce – could they make it ten and secure a place in the Carling Cup semi-final? Sadly, it wasn't to be as bogey team Spurs ended dreams of Wembley with a 2-0 victory at the City of Manchester Stadium. A 1-1 draw at Aston Villa, a controversial 2-2 home draw with Blackburn – where a linesman's decision to overrule his own offside decision cost the hosts their 100% home league record – and a 0-0 draw with Liverpool ended 2007 in satisfactory manner for the Blues, who were still in or around the top six by that point.

P 8 W 1 D 4 L 3 F 9 A 10

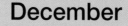

January 2008

City's form continued to slide going into the New Year, despite an impressive 2-0 win at Newcastle two days into 2008. Elano and Gelson Fernandes scored the goals at St James' Park and three days later the Blues returned to Upton Park to hold West Ham 0-0 in the FA Cup third round. Joleon Lescott scored Everton's winner in a game dubbed 'the battle for fourth place' at Goodison Park, but Elano's diving header was enough to put City into the hat for the last 32 in the FA Cup in the replay with West Ham. Four days later the same teams met in the league – their third clash in 15 days – and after a fortuitous 1-1 draw, Sven-Goran Eriksson claimed that he'd had enough of West Ham for one season! An away game against a scratch Sheffield United side would surely see the Blues into the last 16 of the FA Cup, but

thanks to a balloon, it wasn't to be. As Michael Ball went to clear a Sheffield United cross, the ball took a slight deflection off one of the balloons, Ball missed the ball and Sheffield took the lead. A second shortly after meant that Danny Sturridge's second-half effort was no more than a consolation in a morale-sapping

2-1 defeat to the Championship side. A 1-1 with basement side Derby three days later did little to lighten the mood of a disappointing month.

P 7 W 2 D 3 L 2 F 6 A 5

February

Crunch time for the Blues – three league games that would shape the club's Champions League hopes with games against three of the top five clubs in the Premier League. Arsenal became the first side to leave the CoMS with all three points with a 3-1 win over a lacklustre City to start the month, but the highlight of the campaign came eight days later at Old Trafford in the return Manchester derby. Without a win at United since 1974, the Blues' supporters behaved with great dignity during the pre-match silence to mark the 50th anniversary of the Munich air disaster. City then proceeded to tear the Reds apart and goals from Darius Vassell and a debut header from new signing Benjani made it 2-0 by half-time. The Blues continued to dominate after the break and despite Michael Carrick's last-minute goal, City completed their first derby double for 38 years by holding on to win 2-1. A 15-day international break meant that the momentum gathered by that victory had dissipated by the time Everton visited the CoMS and the Toffees thoroughly deserved their 2-0 win.

P 3 W 1 D 0 L 2 F 3 A 6

March

With City still chasing a spot in the UEFA Cup, March was a crucial month for the club, but little would go right for Sven's team. A miserable 0-0 draw with Wigan was followed by a 2-0 defeat to Reading – what had gone wrong? The team had lost their sparkle and needed to re-discover their form quickly if the season wasn't to end flatly and the home visit of Spurs at last gave City fans hope of a late burst for Europe with an impressive 2-1 courtesy of goals from Nedum Onuoha and Martin Petrov. A decent point at Bolton, however, was followed by a hugely disappointing 3-1 defeat at Birmingham City. The Blues had to dust themselves down quickly or miss out on their dream of European football altogether.

P 5 W 1 D 2 L 2 F 3 A 6

April

April proved to be a month of mixed fortunes for City. Chances of a UEFA Cup place had diminished but there was still the possibility of a place in the Intertoto Cup, although Chelsea's comfortable 2-0 win at the CoMS made even that task much harder. Successive wins were the only cure and the Blues did exactly that, winning 2-1 at Sunderland with goals from Elano and a lucky winner from Vassell followed by a sparkling 3-1 win over Portsmouth. Victory over relegation-haunted Fulham would mean City could go into May with a real chance of taking sixth place and with just over 20 minutes gone, goals from Ireland and Benjani put the hosts 2-0 up. In fact, with 70 minutes gone, City still held a two-goal advantage, but a mix of suicidal defending and tiredness allowed the visitors, by then throwing everyone forward, a lifeline and the game turned on its head in the remaining minutes with Fulham completing an amazing comeback to win 3-2. It was a crushing blow for all concerned and meant there was little chance now of finishing in the top six for Sven's men.

P 4 W 2 D 0 L 2 F 7 A 7

May

City ended the season, unusually, with successive away games. A narrow 1-0 defeat at Liverpool meant that, barring a disastrous final day at Middlesbrough, the Blues looked favourites to secure an unlikely UEFA Cup spot via the Fair Play League. Though placed fifth in the Fair Play table, all the teams above City were already in Europe, and only Everton and Fulham could realistically overhaul the Blues. City fans travelled to Middlesbrough in party mood – but were left flabbergasted by events that defied belief. First of all Richard Dunne was sent off after barely 15 minutes, then the Blues capitulated in the remaining 75, conceding eight goals in a humiliating defeat to a side who hadn't scored more than two goals in one game all season. With the news Everton had secured a UEFA Cup spot by finishing fifth, City fans had an agonising wait to discover whether the Blues had done enough to finish higher than Fulham in the Fair Play League. Fortunately, by the narrowest of margins, City finished sixth and qualified for the 2008/09 UEFA Cup. The team finished ninth in the Premier League and a month later Sven-Goran Eriksson was sacked as the Blues' manager.

City of Manchester Stadium Quiz

Can you answer these questions?

1. What is unique about this football?

2. What is this event, watched by 57,000 people?

>> 3. Two of these were introduced in May 2008- what are we talking about?

^^ 4. Where might you find this located?

^^ 5. Gianfranco Zola signs autographs – but why was he at the CoMS?

^^ 6. It looks like a ride from Alton Towers, but what is it really?

^^ 7. Somebody left this in the changing room last season – who does it belong to?

<< 8. A City fan approaches a spaceship? What do you think it is?

Summer Signings: Jo

Brazilian star Jo became the Blues' record signing in July…

João Alves de Assis Silva – or 'Jo' as he prefers, signed for City after the club finally managed to bring the young Brazilian to Manchester. The Blues had been strongly linked with the exciting 21-year-old for several months and though the actual transfer fee remains undisclosed, it is believed to be significantly more than the £13m paid to Paris St Germain for the services of Nicolas Anelka.

Jo will wear the No.14 shirt during the 2008/09 campaign and he will bring a new dimension to City's attack with his power on the ground and in the air, skill and finishing.

Jo's goal scoring record averaged more than one goal every two games during his two-year stay with Russian giants CSKA Moscow. The predominantly left-footed striker was also Mark Hughes' first signing since becoming City manager last June.

"He's a big talent and a young man with a big future," said Hughes. "A lot has been said about him and there was a big expectation on him coming out of Brazil. So with the success he's had I think it's a real coup that we've been able to bring him to the club and I think everybody will enjoy watching him play."

So what do we know about Jo? Well, he was born on March 20, 1987 in Sapopemba, an impoverished neighbourhood of Brazil's largest city, Sao Paulo. After showing plenty of ability as a youngster, he joined Brazilian side Corinthians' academy and eventually broke into the senior side just three years later, quickly establishing himself as a fans' favourite and writing his name into the record books as the club's youngest ever debutant aged 16 years, 3 months and 29 days.

He scored 13 goals in 81 appearances for Corinthians, helping the team to several trophies in the process before moving to Russian side CSKA Moscow, despite rumoured interest from Manchester United, AC Milan, PSV Eindhoven, Benfica and Atletico Madrid.

CSKA Moscow paid £3.5m for Jo in 2006 and he was an instant hit with the fans as his goals helped CSKA sweep all before them domestically over the next two seasons.

He won his only Brazil cap to date during a 0-0 draw with Turkey in June 2007, though he was called up for Brazil's Olympic squad prior to the start of the Premier League.

He scored 44 goals in 77 starts for CSKA, forging a lethal partnership with fellow Brazilian, Wagner Love and earned a reputation for his colourful goal celebration – something City supporters will hope to see plenty of this season.

Jo revealed why he signed by saying, "I decided to come to Manchester City because they showed the most interest in me. I spoke to the manager and I was very pleased with what he said. I was told Manchester City are a club going forward. We can go places together and I decided to come to here for that reason."

City in Europe! 2009

The Blues embark on their ninth European campaign during 2008/09 – to celebrate, here is a map of where all our European opponents have come from, in all competitions...

Northern Ireland:
Linfield (ECWC 1970) 1-2

Denmark:
Gornik Zabrze (1971) 3-1 (ECWC neutral replay)

Wales:
Total Network Solutions (UEFA 2003) 2-0

England:
Chelsea (ECWC 1971) 0-1

Belgium:
SK Lierse (ECWC 1969) 3-0
Standard Liege (UEFA 1978) 0-2
Lokeren (UEFA 2003) 1-0

Spain:
Atletico Bilbao (ECWC 1969) 3-3
Valencia (UEFA 1972) 1-2

Portugal:
Academica Coimbra (ECWC 1970) 0-0

KEY:

EC= European Cup
UEFA = UEFA Cup
ECWC = European Cup
Winners' Cup

Total Away record in European competition:
Pld: 23 W. 6 D. 5 L. 9 F. 23 A. 25

Poland:
Gornik Zabrze (ECWC 1971) 0-2
Widzew Lodz (UEFA 1977) 2-2
Groclin Dyskobolia (UEFA 2003) 0-0

Germany:
Schalke 04 (ECWC 1970) 0-1
Borussia Monchengladbach (UEFA 1979) 1-3

Hungary:
Honved (ECWC 1971) 1-0

Austria:
Gornik Zabrze (1970) 2-1
(ECWC Final)

Turkey:
Fenerbahce (EC 1968) 1-2

Italy:
Juventus (UEFA 1976) 0-1
AC Milan (UEFA 1978) 2-2

Elano

Wordsearch

Look at the letters grid below – can you spot 10 words connected with City? The words could be in order, backwards, diagonal, upwards or downwards – good luck!

```
S D T M D N A K P L C
T B R K O H V K J A B
U X A F O O N I I V H
R W H U F K N C Y A N
R Y N D C A E B M M K
I O W R J D M A E W H
D Y N N O V N C M A B
G M E H T N T N R L M
E B K Q N V O R T E P
M O O N C H E S T E R
K C O R L U K A H J M
```

Answers on page 60/61

Top 10 Goals of the Season

1 – Elano v Newcastle United (September)

GOAL! Only one man would attempt to score with a free-kick from roughly 35-yards out – Elano. The Brazilian hit the ball like a rocket and it flew into the top corner

2 – Geovanni v Manchester United (August)

GOAL! It was going to take something special to pierce United's watertight defence, and it came in the shape of a 25-yard screamer from Geovanni.

3 – Stephen Ireland v Reading (November)

GOAL! With the score at 1-1 and deep into injury time, Samaras headed the ball across the box to Stephen Ireland who volleyed home a powerful shot from the edge of the box.

4 – Michael Johnson v Derby County (August)

GOAL! There seemed little threat when Michael Johnson picked the ball up on the right of midfield, but he cut inside, played a one-two with Elano and hit an exquisite shot into the roof of the net from just inside the box.

5 - Elano v M'brough (October)

GOAL! He'd done it the week before against Newcastle – surely he couldn't do it again? Elano opted for placement rather than power on this occasion and curled a 20-yard free-kick into the top left-hand corner.

6 – Daniel Sturridge v Sheffield Utd (January)

GOAL! The only bright spot of a forgettable afternoon – substitute Danny Sturridge's sublime volley, in off the crossbar, to give the Blues hope against Sheffield United.

7 – Darius Vassell v Man U (February)

GOAL! Not so much spectacular as enjoyable, Vassell found himself in space in the United box and fired a volley, which seemed to be going wide – but it was saved by the keeper and he made no mistake with the rebound.

8 – Gelson Fernandes v Newcastle Utd (January)

GOAL! A terrific strike by City's Swiss international midfielder, who finished emphatically to give the Blues a vital second away to Newcastle.

9 – Elano v Middlesbrough (May)

GOAL! With all seemingly lost and City 7-0 down, substitute Elano picked the ball up and decided to take on the Middlesbrough defence single-handedly – and it worked as he curled in a delightful consolation goal.

10 – Elano v Middlesbrough (October)

GOAL! Middlesbrough must be sick of the sight of Elano! Six of his 10 goals last season came against clubs from the north east – this effort was a lovely volley from the edge of the box and his first of three goals against Boro during the campaign.

Champion Blues

City's Academy side lifted the FA Youth Cup for the first time in 21 years last April…

With almost 20,000 packing into the City of Manchester Stadium for the second leg of the 2008 FA Youth Cup final last month, the young Blues produced a super display to lift the most prestigious cup in youth football.

It was an evening that crackled with excitement from start to finish and there were thrills, spills and goals as the boy Blues completed a wonderful season by adding the cup to the league title they'd won several weeks earlier.

After seeing off Millwall, Reading, Bristol City and Plymouth, City took on Chelsea in the two-legged final. Poised evenly at 1-1 from the first leg at Stamford Bridge, it was Chelsea who drew first blood at the City of Manchester Stadium, with Ryan McGivern unluckily deflecting a Greg Hartley save past his own keeper on six minutes.

But the Blues, inspired by skipper Ben Mee, equalised on 24 minutes with Mee himself heading home Andrew Tutte's superb back post cross.

The quick-footed Slovakian winger Vladimir Weiss showed the City fans why he's so highly-regarded

MATCH FACTS:

CITY:
Hartley, Trippier (Ibrahim 90, McGivern, Boyata (Tsiaklis 82), Mee, Tutte, Weiss, Kay, Ball, Mak, McDermott.
Not used: Mentel, Nimely and Poole.

CHELSEA:
Taylor, Nana, Vantdhmoet, Aanholt, Gordon (Nouble 72), Woods, Stoch, Mellis, Nielsen (Philip 54), Rodriguez and Kakuta, Saville.

REFEREE:
Peter Walton

ATTENDANCE:
19,783

with a stunning 20-yard free-kick to put the Blues 2-1 ahead on 35 minutes and it was Weiss' pace and trickery that won a late penalty, which David Ball converted to the delight of the home fans.

There was still enough time for Chelsea's Jacob Mellis to be red-carded for a reckless challenge on Kieran Trippier, but the young defender's injury was nowhere near as bad as first feared and he was able to join the celebrations at the end of the match.

Proud Academy chief Jim Cassell said: "It was the best feeling of my life, football-wise. It was something we've wanted to do for many years. We felt we could have won it on other occasions, but didn't, so when it did finally come along it was all the sweeter. I thought the players were absolutely outstanding.

"We've achieved something we'd set out to do and this is the icing on the cake to win the FA Youth Cup. The supporters were fantastic and I can't say how pleased and proud we were of them. Everyone within the club should be applauded for making it such a special night. Now we have to ensure we stay on top and so the hard work will continue."

BigCityQuiz 2009

Can you qualify for Europe? Can you maybe even win the league? Or will you end up in the relegation zone? Below are 38 questions representing a league season for the Blues – you get three points for a correct answer and occasionally, you'll get a point for 'HOME' answers and three points for 'AWAY' answers – which are a bit tougher. See how many points you can collect and then find out whether you've done enough to ensure another season in charge or are facing the sack….

1 – HOME:
Who was City's top scorer last season?

2 – AWAY:
Which teams did Danny Sturridge score goals against last season?

3 – HOME:
Who are the only two teams City failed to score against last season both home and away?

4 – AWAY:
How many City players were sent off last season?

5 – HOME:
Who did Kasper Schmeichel make his City debut against?

6 – AWAY:
Who did Valeri Bojinov start his only game for City against last season?

7 – HOME:
Who knocked City out of the Carling Cup last season?

8 – AWAY:
Which team did the Blues meet five times in league and cup matches last season?

9 – HOME:
Which foreign player claimed his mum liked Manchester so much, she wanted to move here!

10 – AWAY:
Which country do Vladimir Weiss and Robbie Mak come from?

11 – HOME:
True or false? City's biggest home gate last season was against Arsenal

12 – AWAY:
What is the name of City's kit manager?

13 – HOME:
Who did the Blues beat in the 2008 FA Youth Cup Final?

14 – AWAY:
What was the aggregate score in the above game?

15 – HOME:
Who did City play in the 2007 Thomas Cook Trophy?

16 – AWAY:
Which team did Georgios Samaras score his only City goal against last season?

17 – HOME:
Which team did Samaras sign for City from?

18 – AWAY:
Who did Mark Hughes manage before Blackburn Rovers?

19 – HOME:
How many goals did Benjani score for City last season?

20 – AWAY:
Andreas Isaksson played six times last season – how many goals did he concede in total? A) 10 B) 12 C) 14

21 – HOME:
Who joined City from Fiorentina?

22 – AWAY:
Which player slightly deflected Geovanni's winning goal against Manchester United?

23 – HOME:
Who scored City's fastest goal of last season?

24 – AWAY:
Who signed for City from Real Sociedad?

25 – HOME:
Which City player joined Lazio on loan in January 2008?

26 – AWAY:
What is the total amount of goals City scored and conceded last season in the Premier League?
A) 98 B) 101 C) 103

27 – HOME:
Who scored City's first home goal of 2007/08?

28 – AWAY:
City qualified for the UEFA Cup via the Fair Play League – but where did the Blues finish in the Fair Play table? A) 5th B) 6th C) 7th

29 – HOME:
Which City player was born in Birmingham but raised in Leeds?

30 – AWAY:
Which three teams did City complete the league double over last season?

31 – HOME:
Who are the only two City players to have scored more than one goal in a game last season?

32 – AWAY:
How many clean sheets did Joe Hart keep for City last season in all competitions? A) 5 B) 8 C) 10

33 – HOME:
Which Academy defender made his only City appearance when he came on as a substitute against Portsmouth last season?

34 – AWAY:
What score was it at half-time when City played Middlesbrough away last season?

35 – HOME:
Who scored his first senior goal against Tottenham last season?

36 – AWAY:
Who made his debut against Norwich City in the Carling Cup and then joined them on loan?

37 – HOME:
Which two clubs did Paul Dickov go out on loan to last season?

38 – AWAY:
City only managed to score four goals in a league game once last season – who was it against?

How did you score?

90 points or more – Congratulations! You've won the title!
75-89 – Champions League football – well done!
65-74 – UEFA Cup football – great season!
50-64 – Mid-table finish – not too bad!
40-49 – You just escaped relegation…
Less than 40 points – Get your coat… you're fired!

Who is celebrating?

Can you guess, just from looking at a portion of a player's body who is celebrating a goal? One point for the scorer, two bonus points if you get the game, too…

Answers on page 60/61

Crossword

Answer the questions, and fill in the blanks
and see if you can complete the puzzle.

Across

1 The Blues' Bulgarian winger (5, 6)
4 Striker signed from Portsmouth last season (7)
7 City's top scorer last season (5)
9 Head of the Academy (3, 7)
10 England's No. 1 (3, 4)
12 City defender born in Nigeria (5, 6)
15 Name of City's triumphant Academy skipper (3, 3)
16 He scored on his debut for Wales (4, 5)
17 City chairman Dr Thaksin Shinawatra was born here (8)
18 City's Swiss midfielder (6, 9)

Down

1 City's England defender (5, 8)
2 Slovakian winger who scored in the FA Youth Cup final (8, 5)
3 Mark Hughes' assistant manager (4, 5)
5 Club mascot! (11)
6 City fans sing this song during every home game (4, 4)
8 The Blues' new manager (4, 6)
11 City's Player of the Year 2007/08 (7, 5)
13 He scored the winning goal against United in last season's home derby (8)
14 The Blues' new executive chairman (5, 4)
16 Vedran Corluka plays international football for ? (7)

Derby Delight!

It was the derby day double to end them all – a 1-0 victory at the City of Manchester Stadium followed by a 2-1 win at Old Trafford – here are a collection of images from two unforgettable days...

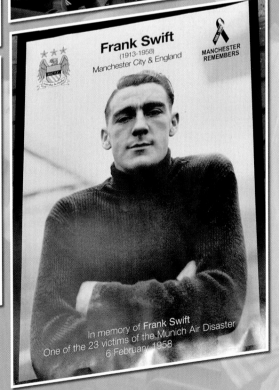

Frank Swift
(1913-1958)
Manchester City & England

MANCHESTER REMEMBERS

In memory of Frank Swift
One of the 23 victims of the Munich Air Disaster
6 February 1958

Profile: Joe Hart

Manchester City & England

FACTFILE:

Born:
19/4/87

Birthplace:
Shrewsbury Town

Height:
6' 3"

Weight:
12st 9lbs

Previous clubs:
Shrewsbury Town,
Tranmere (loan),
Blackpool (loan)

Honours:
England Under-19
(5 caps), England
Under-21 (11 caps),
England (1 cap)

When England boss Fabio Cappello and current national team No.1 David James tip you as the future of English goalkeeping, you know you must be doing something right. Joe Hart's emergence from reserve team keeper to England international inside 12 months has been nothing short of incredible and, of course, there is much more to come from the Blues' talented custodian.

Hart began his career with his hometown club Shrewsbury Town, making his debut one day after his 17th birthday against Gravesend in the Conference and made six appearances the following season. After that, he became first choice goalkeeper at Gay Meadow and was soon attracting the attention of top Premier League clubs, but it was City who made Shrewsbury an offer they couldn't refuse, paying £600,000 in May 2006.

He made his City debut five months later during a 0-0 draw with Sheffield United but it wasn't until the 2007/08 season that Hart finally won a permanent starting place for the Blues, edging out Andreas Isaksson and Kasper Schmeichel for the coveted No.1 jersey.

Hart had, by that time, already represented his country numerous times at Under-19 and Under-21 level and his consistency during his first Premier League season, plus several breathtaking saves throughout the campaign, particularly at Bristol City, Portsmouth and Liverpool, earned him the City supporters' Young Player of the Year award.

"The fans have been brilliant to me ever since I came here," said Hart. "I'm pretty sure no-one had ever heard of me when I made my debut but when I got my first touch they were right behind me. From then it's been excellent so I want to thank them."

There was even better to come for Hart when he was included in the senior England side against the USA and though he remained on the bench for that game, he came on as a second half substitute against Trinidad and Tobago a few days later.

Athletic, acrobatic and confident, Hart looks set to follow in the footsteps of great City goalkeepers such as Bert Trautmann, Frank Swift and Joe Corrigan and is likely to keep goal for the Blues for many years to come.

Young and in love.

LIVE4CITY is the FREE seasonal membership for all young fans who love City. Join up for access to great benefits such as match tickets for £5 and your chance to train at our Platt Lane Academy.

Sign up now at LIVE4CITY.co.uk and receive your FREE membership pack.

LIVE4CITY

RE
IG
CUNIANS

M.C.F.C.
Superbia In Proelio

Ones2Watch2009

Who are the next big things from City's Academy? Here, we look at the most promising youngsters emerging from the youth team...

KIERAN TRIPPIER

>>

A Manchester lad, Kieran Trippier is a highly-rated full-back who is expected to challenge for a first team spot in the next year or so. Blessed with pace and excellent technique, Trippier is a natural attack-minded defender and is another member of last season's FA Youth Cup-winning squad.

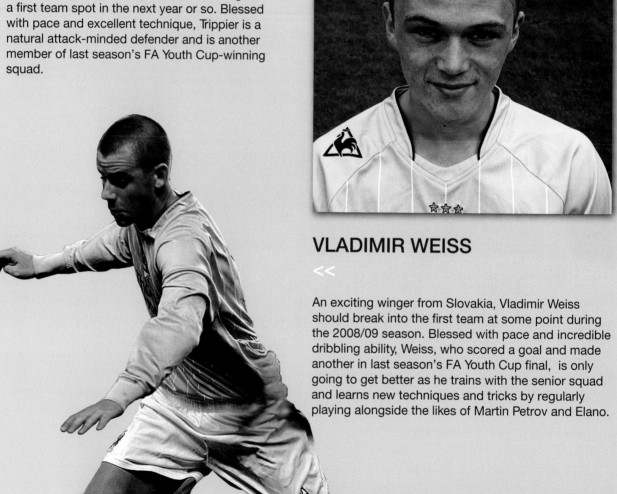

VLADIMIR WEISS

<<

An exciting winger from Slovakia, Vladimir Weiss should break into the first team at some point during the 2008/09 season. Blessed with pace and incredible dribbling ability, Weiss, who scored a goal and made another in last season's FA Youth Cup final, is only going to get better as he trains with the senior squad and learns new techniques and tricks by regularly playing alongside the likes of Martin Petrov and Elano.

DANNY STURRIDGE

>>

Danny Sturridge is somebody most City fans already know plenty about. Injuries kept the Academy striker out of action for much of 2007, but he showed, when given the opportunity, that he is more than ready for a run in the first team. A gifted individual, he is capable of scoring out of nothing, whether that means firing in a rocket shot from 30 yards or volleying home from 20 yards – he can do it all and seems destined for great things in the next few years.

CHED EVANS

<<

With former Wales national team boss Mark Hughes now in charge at City, Ched Evans could well be a player to emerge from the fringes of the first team this season. The prolific Academy and reserve team striker has taken his chance to impress while out on loan at Norwich during 2007/08. He scored 10 goals for the Canaries, a hat-trick for Wales Under-21s and then a goal on his senior Wales debut! Hughes will be well aware of the young Welshman's ability.

Tal Ben Haim

Tal Ben Haim became Mark Hughes' second summer signing when he joined City from Chelsea. The Israeli international spent a year at Stamford Bridge after leaving Bolton Wanderers on a free transfer.

The 26-year-old defender signed a four-year contract for an undisclosed fee and Tal can play in either central defence or as a full-back. He first made his name with Israeli side Maccabi Tel Aviv before moving to the Reebok Stadium in 2004 for a fee of just £150,000.

He was an integral member of Sam Allardyce's Bolton team, but when Jose Mourinho offered him the chance to play for Chelsea, he didn't hesitate. Despite assurances of first-team football with the London Blues, he only started 14 games with Ricardo Carvalho and John Terry the preferred centre-back pairing. His opportunities to shine were few and far between, even when former Israel manager Avram Grant took the reins from Mourinho. With another change of manager at Chelsea, Ben Haim felt the time was right to move on and when City came in with an offer, he was only too happy to accept.

"Manchester City is a very good club and a very famous one, too," said Ben Haim. "I want to win things with this club - I know for many years that hasn't happened. It will be hard because it takes time to build something.

"I know Mark Hughes matches my ambition. As a player he won nearly everything and, of course, he wants to do the same as a manager. He has ambition, the passion and the desire to be successful and that matches my own ambition.

"I know Manchester very well because I used to live here for three years when I was with Bolton so I know that the weather can be a little cold, but the people are very warm – so it's good for me because it's like coming back home.

"I know the City fans are incredible and the support they give to the players creates a fantastic atmosphere. They deserve the best and, hopefully, we can bring them success. The manager wants to build something good here and I'm proud to be here.

"I'm definitely going to give my best to City and give my heart in every game. I hope that we can do good things this season and I can't wait to get started."

Ben Haim, who has served in the Israeli Defence Force, is the second Israeli to play for the Blues, following in Eyal Berkovic's footsteps – and if he proves to be even half as popular as Eyal, his time with City will be an extremely happy one.

Elano

Can you spot the ball?

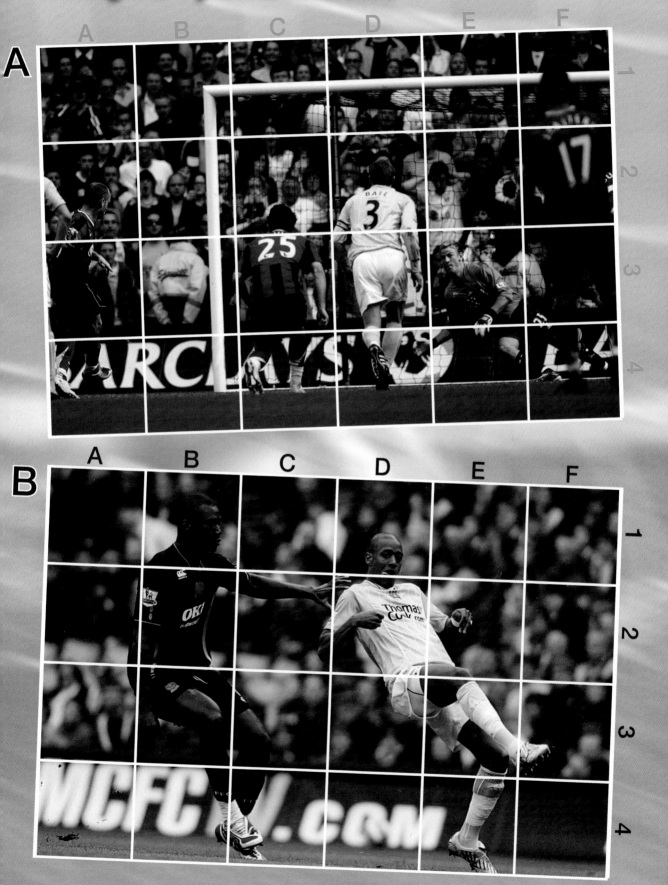

Answers on page 60/61

Profile: Micah Richards

Manchester City & England

FACTFILE:

Born:
24/6/88

Birthplace:
Birmingham

Weight:
13 st 8 lbs

Height:
5' 11"

Previous clubs:
Oldham Athletic
(youth)

Honours:
England Under-16,
England Under-19,
England Under-21,
England (12 caps)

Injury prevented Micah Richards furthering his reputation for club and country and the Academy defender will be keen to get back on track during the new season. He will first want to impress on new manager Mark Hughes that his ideal position is centre-back and then he will aim to regain his England place by impressing Fabio Cappello – Micah missed the first three internationals under Cappello due to injury.

Of course, Micah, who won 12 caps under Steve McClaren, plays his international football at right-back, as he has done for City, though many believe he will one day play centre-back for his country, too. He proved what a threat he can be going forward for England by setting up Frank Lampard to score against Germany and then powering home his first international goal against Israel.

He was nominated for the PFA Young Player of the Year award for a second year in succession and signed a new five-and-a-half year deal that means he will be a City player until June 2013 – one of the longest and most lucrative contracts in the Blues' history.

Micah, who has also represented England at Under-16, Under-19 and Under-21 level, said, "I've always wanted to be at this club and signing such a long contract proves that." The Birmingham-born star will aim to top 100 appearances for City next season, by which time he will reach the grand old age of 20! He will also hope to add a few more goals to his game, too, having managed just two so far, both being equalisers deep into injury time during matches played away from home.

A powerhouse defender, excellent in the air and crunching in the tackle, Blues' boss Mark Hughes is likely to want to build his team around players like Micah Richards who has naturally become one of the most sought-after defenders in Europe – the club, however, will fight tooth and nail to ensure he remains a City player for many, many years.

Manchester City Squad Stats
2009

JOE HART

No: 25
Position: Goalkeeper
Date of birth: 19/04/87
Place of birth: Shrewsbury
Height: 6' 5"
Previous clubs: Shrewsbury Town, Blackpool (loan), Tranmere (loan)
Signed: May 2006
Fee: £600,000

KASPER SCHMEICHEL

No: 19
Position: Goalkeeper
Date of birth: 05/11/86
Place of birth: Denmark
Height: 6' 0"
Previous clubs: Darlington (loan), Bury (loan), Falkirk (loan), Cardiff City (loan), Coventry City (loan)
Signed: Academy
Fee: £0

RICHARD DUNNE

No: 22
Position: Defender
Date of birth: 21/09/79
Place of birth: Dublin, Ireland
Height: 6' 2"
Previous clubs: Everton
Signed: October 2000
Fee: £3m

NEDUM ONUOHA

No: 4
Position: Defender
Date of birth: 12/11/86
Place of birth:
Warri, Nigeria
Height: 6' 0"
Previous clubs: None
Signed: Academy
Fee: £0

MICAH RICHARDS

No: 2
Position: Defender
Date of birth: 24/06/88
Place of birth:
Birmingham
Height: 5' 11"
Previous clubs: Oldham
(youth)
Signed: Academy
Fee: £0

STEPHEN IRELAND

No: 7
Position: Midfielder
Date of birth: 22/08/86
Place of birth:
Cork, Ireland
Height: 5' 8"
Previous clubs: None
Signed: Academy
Fee: £0

Manchester City Squad Stats
2009

DARIUS VASSELL

No: 12
Position: Striker
Date of birth: 30/06/80
Place of birth: Birmingham
Height: 5' 9"
Previous clubs: Aston Villa
Signed: July 2005
Fee: £2m

MICHAEL BALL

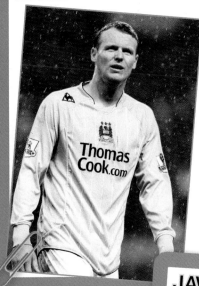

No: 3
Position: Defender
Date of birth: 02/10/79
Place of birth: Liverpool
Height: 5' 10"
Previous clubs: Everton, Rangers, PSV Eindhoven
Signed: Jan 2007
Fee: Undisclosed

JAVIER GARRIDO

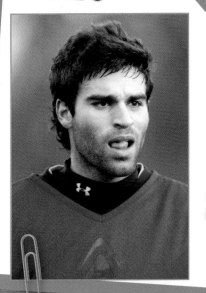

No: 24
Position: Defender
Date of birth: 15/03/85
Place of birth: Irun, Spain
Height: 5' 11"
Previous clubs: Real Sociedad
Signed: July 2007
Fee: £1.5m

ELANO

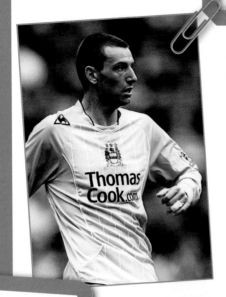

No: 11
Position: Midfielder
Date of birth: 14/06/81
Place of birth: Iracemápolis
Height: 5' 09"
Previous clubs: SC Gurani, Internacional, Santos, America (loan), Shakhtar Donetsk
Signed: July 2007
Fee: £8m

MICHAEL JOHNSON

No: 6
Position: Midfielder
Date of birth: 24/02/88
Place of birth: Manchester
Height: 6' 0"
Previous clubs: Feyenoord (junior)
Signed: Academy
Fee: £0

MARTIN PETROV

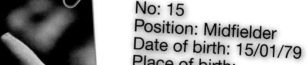

No: 15
Position: Midfielder
Date of birth: 15/01/79
Place of birth: Vratsa, Bulgaria
Height: 6' 1"
Previous clubs: CSKA Sofia, Servette, Wolfsburg, Atletico Madrid
Signed: July 2007
Fee: £4.7m

Manchester City Squad Stats
2009

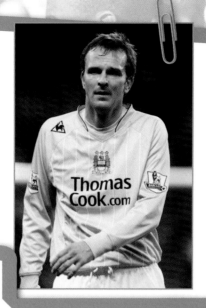

DIETMAR HAMANN

No: 21
Position: Midfielder
Date of birth: 27/08/73
Place of birth:
Waldsasson, Germany
Height: 6' 3"
Previous clubs: Bayern
Munich, Newcastle,
Liverpool, Bolton
Signed: July 2006
Fee: £400,000

VEDRAN CORLUKA

No: 16
Position: Defender
Date of birth: 05/02/86
Place of birth:
Doboj, Bosnia
Height: 6' 3"
Previous clubs: Dinamo
Zagreb, Inter Zapresic
(loan)
Signed: July 2007
Fee: £8.9m (approx)

GELSON FERNANDES

No: 28
Position: Midfielder
Date of birth: 02/09/86
Place of birth:
Praia, Cape Verde
Height: 6' 0"
Previous clubs: FC Sion
Signed: July 2007
Fee: Undisclosed

VALERI BOJINOV

No: 29
Position: Striker
Date of birth: 15/02/86
Place of birth:
Oriahovizca, Bulgaria
Height: 5' 10"
Previous clubs:
Fiorentina, Juventus
(loan)
Signed: July 2007
Fee: Undisclosed

FELIPE CAICEDO

No: 20
Position: Striker
Date of birth: 05/09/88
Place of birth:
Guayaquil, Ecuador
Height: 6' 1"
Previous clubs:
Rocafuerte, FC Basle
Signed: Jan 2008
Fee: £5.2m

MWARUWARI BENJANI

No: 27
Position: Striker
Date of birth: 13/08/78
Place of birth:
Bulawayo, Zimbabwe
Height: 6' 2"
Previous clubs: Jomo
Cosmos, Grasshoppers
Zurich, Auxerre,
Portsmouth
Signed: Feb 2008
Fee: £3.87m

CHED EVANS

No: 33
Position: Striker
Date of birth: 28/12/88
Place of birth:
Rhyl
Height: 6' 1"
Previous clubs:
Norwich City (loan)
Signed: Academy
Fee: £0

DANIEL STURRIDGE

No: 36
Position: Striker
Date of birth: 01/09/88
Place of birth:
Birmingham
Height: 6' 0"
Previous clubs: None
Signed: Academy
Fee: £0

SHALEUM LOGAN

No: 38
Position: Defender
Date of birth: 06/11/88
Place of birth:
Manchester
Height: 6' 1"
Previous clubs:
Scunthorpe (loan),
Grimsby (loan),
Stockport County (loan)
Signed: Academy
Fee: £0

Guess Who?

Can you work out who these City players are?
We've disguised them by one means or another so
you'll have to use a bit of detective work…

Mark II!

Mark Bowen became City's new assistant manager during the summer – here is the low-down on Mark Hughes' number two...

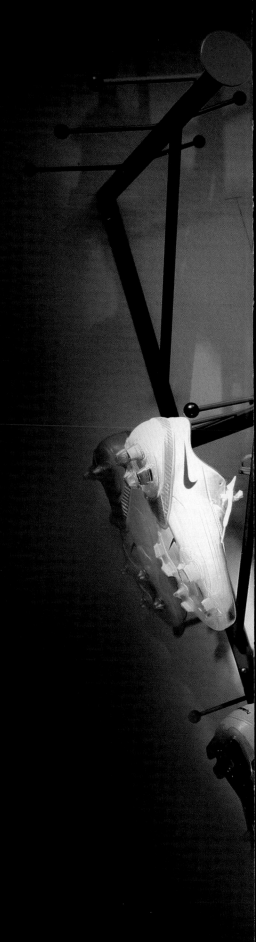

Born in Neath, South Wales in 1963, Mark Bowen began his career with Tottenham Hotspur in 1981, but he never managed to establish himself during his six years in North London, making just 17 starts.

There was interest from several clubs – including Manchester City – but Bowen eventually opted for the promise of first-team football with Norwich City, where he would spend nine happy years.

One of the most reliable defenders in the country, Bowen made 399 appearances for the Canaries – a disagreement with new manager Gary Megson prevented him making it 400 - before moving on to West Ham United, Charlton and Reading.

During Bowen's time with Norwich, he became a regular Wales international and would go on to represent his country 41 times. He once scored for Norwich in a famous 2-1 UEFA Cup win away to Bayern Munich as the Canaries became the only British side to ever beat them on their own soil.

After Norwich, he moved to West Ham, making 20 appearances for the Hammers before joining Japanese side Shimizu Pulse, managed by former Tottenham legend Ossie Ardiles in March 1997. He returned to England six months later, joining Charlton Athletic and ironically made his debut against to Norwich, of all clubs, helping his new club to a dramatic 4-0 win at Carrow Road.

Bowen's experience played a big part in helping the Addicks to the 1998 play-off final against Sunderland and in one of the most memorable finals the old stadium had ever seen, the see-saw game ended 4-4 and Bowen successfully converted a penalty in the resulting shoot-out that took Charlton into the Premiership for the first time.

By then aged 36, a groin injury meant he missed most of the 1998/99 campaign and it was around that time that he first considered moving into the coaching and management side of the game.

After meeting his old friend Mark Hughes at a coaching course, Bowen was invited to help out with the Wales Under-21 team following Hughes' appointment as national team manager. Still registered with Charlton, he was released and had brief spells with Bristol City, Oxford and Wigan Athletic before finishing his career with Reading.

He continued with Wales and then moved to Blackburn Rovers to become Hughes' second in command. Along with first team coach Eddie Niedzwiecki, they turned Rovers into one of the toughest sides to beat in the Premier League.

Now Bowen, who has a reputation for being firm but fair, is aiming to help City to new heights in the coming years by helping the squad achieve maximum levels of fitness and effort – watch out for him barking instructions out in the technical area this season!

Date	Opponent	ATT	Score	Starting Line-up	Subs Used
AUGUST					
11	West Ham	34,921	2-0	Schmeichel Corluka Garrido Dunne Richards Elano Hamann Ireland Johnson Petrov **Bianchi**	Bojinov Onuoha **Geovanni**
15	**Derby County**	43,620	**1-0**	Schmeichel Corluka Garrido Dunne Richards Elano Hamann Ireland **Johnson** Petrov Bianchi	Bojinov Geovanni
19	**Man United**	44,995	**1-0**	Schmeichel Corluka Garrido Dunne Richards Elano Hamann Bojinov Johnson Petrov **Geovanni**	Ball Mpenza Bianchi
25	Arsenal	60,114	0-1	Schmeichel Corluka Garrido Dunne Richards Elano Hamann Ireland Johnson Petrov Mpenza	Ball Geovanni Bianchi
29	Bristol City (CC2)	14,541	2-1	Hart Corluka Ball Sun Onuoha Gelson Logan Ireland **Bianchi** **Mpenza** Geovanni	Dickov Dabo
SEPTEMBER					
02	Blackburn Rovers	26,881	0-1	Schmeichel Corluka Garrido Dunne Richards Elano Hamann Ireland Johnson Petrov Bianchi	Mpenza Geovanni Onuoha
16	**Aston Villa**	38,363	**1-0**	Schmeichel Corluka Garrido Onuoha Richards Elano Hamann Vassell **Johnson** Petrov Mpenza	Ball Sun Bianchi
22	Fulham	24,674	3-3	Schmeichel Corluka Garrido Dunne Richards Elano Hamann Ireland Johnson Petrov2 Mpenza	Sun Geovanni Bianchi
25	Norwich (CC3)	20,938	1-0	Hart Onuoha Ball Dunne Sun Gelson Logan Ireland Bianchi **Samaras** Geovanni	Evans Etuhu
29	**Newcastle United**	40,606	**3-1**	Hart Corluka Garrido Dunne Richards Elano Hamann Ireland Johnson **Petrov** Mpenza	Ball Geovanni Onuoha
OCTOBER					
07	**Middlesbrough**	40,348	**3-1**	Hart Corluka Garrido Dunne Richards **Elano2** Hamann Ireland Johnson Petrov Mpenza	Ball Geovanni Samaras
20	**Birmingham City**	45,688	**1-0**	Hart Corluka Garrido Dunne Richards **Elano** Hamann Ireland Johnson Petrov Mpenza	Ball Gelson Samaras
27	Chelsea	41,832	0-6	Hart Corluka Garrido Dunne Richards Elano Hamann Ireland Johnson Petrov Samaras	Ball Vassell Bianchi
31	Bolton (CC4)	15,501	1-0	Isaksson Corluka Garrido Dunne Richards **ElanoP** Hamann Ireland Johnson Ball Samaras	Vassell Onuoha Gelson
NOVEMBER					
05	**Sunderland**	40,038	**1-0**	Hart Corluka Garrido Dunne Sun Elano Hamann **Ireland** Johnson Petrov Mpenza	Ball Vassell Bianchi
11	Portsmouth	19,529	0-0	Hart Corluka Garrido Dunne Richards Elano Hamann Ireland Gelson Petrov Vassell	Bianchi Geovanni
24	**Reading**	43,813	**2-1**	Isaksson Corluka Garrido Dunne Richards Elano Hamann **Ireland** Gelson **Petrov** Mpenza	Geovanni Samaras Sun
DECEMBER					
01	Wigan Athletic	18,614	1-1	Isaksson Corluka Garrido Dunne Richards Gelson Hamann Ireland Samaras Petrov **Geovanni**	Ball Etuhu Bianchi
09	Spurs	35,646	1-2	Isaksson Corluka Garrido Dunne Richards Gelson Johnson Ireland Etuhu Petrov Vassell	**Bianchi** Geovanni
15	**Bolton**	40,506	**4-2**	Isaksson Corluka Ball Dunne Richards Hamann Johnson Gelson **Bianchi** Petrov **Vassell**	**Etuhu** Garrido Mpenza
18	Spurs (CC5)	38,564	0-2	Hart Corluka Garrido Dunne Richards Hamann Johnson Elano Bianchi Petrov Vassell	Mpenza Geovanni Ball
22	Aston Villa	41,455	1-1	Hart Onuoha Ball Dunne Richards Gelson Hamann Elano **Bianchi** Petrov Vassell	Etuhu Garrido Corluka
27	**Blackburn**	42,112	**2-2**	Hart Onuoha Ball Dunne Richards Gelson Ireland Corluka Bianchi Petrov **Vassell**	Elano Garrido
30	**Liverpool**	47,321	**0-0**	Hart Onuoha Ball Dunne Richards Elano Ireland Corluka Hamann Petrov Vassell	Bianchi Geovanni Gelson
JANUARY 2008					
02	Newcastle	50,956	2-0	Hart Onuoha Ball Dunne Richards **Elano** Ireland Corluka Hamann Petrov Vassell	**Gelson** Etuhu Bianchi
05	West Ham (FAC3)	33,806	0-0	Hart Onuoha Ball Dunne Richards Castillo Ireland Corluka Hamann Petrov Vassell	Gelson Etuhu Bianchi
12	Everton	38,474	0-1	Hart Onuoha Ball Dunne Richards Elano Castillo Corluka Hamann Petrov Vassell	Gelson Ireland Bianchi
16	West Ham (FAC3R)	27,809	1-0	Hart Corluka Ball Dunne Richards **Elano** Castillo Ireland Hamann Petrov Vassell	Gelson Bianchi
20	**West Ham**	39,042	**1-1**	Hart Corluka Ball Dunne Richards Elano Castillo Ireland Hamann Petrov **Vassell**	Gelson Garrido Geovanni
27	Sheff Utd (FAC4)	20,800	1-2	Hart Onuoha Ball Dunne Corluka Elano Gelson Mpenza Hamann Petrov Vassell	Ireland **Sturridge** Geovanni
30	Derby County	31,368	1-1	Hart Sun Ball Dunne Corluka Etuhu Gelson Ireland **Sturridge** Petrov Vassell	Elano Geovanni Mpenza
FEBRUARY					
02	**Arsenal**	46,426	**1-3**	Hart Corluka Ball Dunne Richards Elano **Gelson** Hamann Petrov Sturridge Ireland	Mpenza Geovanni Vassell
10	Manchester Utd	75,970	2-1	Hart Onuoha Ball Dunne Richards Gelson Hamann Ireland Petrov **Benjani** **Vassell**	Sun Garrido Caicedo
25	**Everton**	41,728	**0-2**	Hart Onuoha Ball Dunne Richards Gelson Hamann Ireland Petrov Benjani Vassell	Elano Caicedo Castillo
MARCH					
01	**Wigan Athletic**	38,261	**0-0**	Hart Onuoha Ball Dunne Corluka Gelson Johnson Ireland Elano Benjani Vassell	Caicedo Castillo
08	Reading	24,062	0-2	Hart Garrido Ball Dunne Corluka Gelson Johnson Hamann Elano Benjani Vassell	Caicedo Castillo Sun
16	**Spurs**	40,180	**2-1**	Hart Garrido **Onuoha** Dunne Corluka Gelson Johnson Castillo Elano Benjani **Ireland**	Caicedo Sun Vassell
22	Bolton Wanderers	22,633	0-0	Hart Garrido Onuoha Dunne Corluka Gelson Johnson Petrov Vassell Benjani Ireland	Caicedo Elano
29	Birmingham City	22,962	1-3	Hart Garrido Onuoha Dunne Onuoha Gelson Hamann **ElanoP** Vassell Benjani Ireland	Caicedo Geovanni Mpenza
APRIL					
05	**Chelsea**	42,594	**0-2**	Hart Ball Onuoha Dunne Onuoha Gelson Ireland Elano Petrov Benjani Johnson	Sun Caicedo Vassell
12	Sunderland	46,797	2-1	Hart Ball Corluka Dunne Sun Gelson Ireland **ElanoP** Petrov Benjani Johnson	Sturridge **Vassell** Hamann
20	**Portsmouth**	40,205	**3-1**	Hart Ball Corluka Dunne Ireland Gelson **Vassell** Elano Petrov Benjani Johnson	Geovanni Caicedo Williamson
26	**Fulham**	43,634	**2-3**	Hart Ball Corluka Sun **Ireland** Gelson Vassell Elano Petrov Benjani Johnson	Geovanni Caicedo
MAY					
04	Liverpool	43,074	0-1	Hart Sun Corluka Dunne Ireland Johnson Vassell Elano Petrov Benjani Ball	Castillo Garrido Hamann
11	Middlesbrough	27,613	1-8	Isaksson Sun Corluka Dunne Ireland Garrido Vassell Gelson Petrov Benjani Ball	**Elano** Castillo Hamann

HOME AWAY | PREMIERSHIP CARLING CUP FA CUP | ► YELLOW CARD ► RED CARD | **ELANO** = GOALSCORER | ELANO P = PENALTY SCORED

Player	(Premier Lg)		(Cup Comps)		Totals	
	Apps	Gls	Apps	Gls	Apps	Gls
Andreas Isaksson	5	0	1	0	6	0
Kasper Schmeichel	7	0	0	0	7	0
Joe Hart	26	0	6	0	32	0
Michael Ball	19 (9)	0	6 (1)	0	25 (10)	0
Micah Richards	25	0	4	0	29	0
Nedum Onuoha	13 (3)	1	4 (1)	0	17 (4)	1
Vedran Corluka	34 (1)	0	6	0	40 (1)	0
Jihai Sun	7 (7)	0	2	0	9 (7)	0
Richard Dunne	36	0	6	0	42	0
Javier Garrido	21 (6)	0	2	0	23 (6)	0
Sam Williamson	0 (1)	0	0	0	0 (1)	0
Shaleum Logan	0	0	2	0	2	0
Ousmane Dabo	0	0	0 (1)	0	0 (1)	0
Michael Johnson	23	2	2	0	25	2
Dietmar Hamann	26 (3)	0	5	0	31 (3)	0
Gelson Fernandes	21 (5)	2	3 (3)	0	24 (8)	2
Stephen Ireland	32 (1)	4	5 (1)	0	37 (2)	4
Geovanni	2 (17)	3	2 (2)	0	4 (19)	3
Elano	29 (3)	8	4	2	33 (3)	10
Martin Petrov	34	5	4	0	38	5
Nery Castillo	2 (5)	0	2	0	4 (5)	0
Kelvin Etuhu	2 (4)	1	0 (2)	0	2 (6)	1
Emile Mpenza	8 (7)	2	2 (1)	1	10 (8)	3
Rolando Bianchi	7 (12)	4	3 (2)	1	10 (14)	5
Darius Vassell	21 (5)	6	4 (1)	0	25 (6)	6
Paul Dickov	0	0	0 (1)	0	0 (1)	0
Georgios Samaras	2 (3)	0	2	1	4 (3)	1
Benjani Mwaruwari	13	3	0	0	13	3
Valeri Bojinov	1 (2)	0	0	0	1 (2)	0
Ched Evans	0	0	0 (1)	0	0 (1)	0
Danny Sturridge	2 (1)	1	0 (1)	1	2 (2)	2
Felipe Caicedo	0 (10)	0	0	0	0 (10)	0

	Pld	W	D	L	F	A	PTS	Euro Qual
01. Manchester Utd	38	27	6	5	80	22	87	CLg
02. Chelsea	38	25	10	3	65	26	85	CLg
03. Arsenal	38	24	11	3	74	31	83	CLg
04. Liverpool	38	21	13	4	67	28	76	CLg
05. Everton	38	19	8	11	55	33	65	UEFA Cup
06. Aston Villa	38	16	12	10	71	51	60	Intertoto
07. Blackburn Rovers	38	15	13	10	50	48	58	
08. Portsmouth	38	16	9	13	48	40	57	UEFA Cup
09. Manchester City	38	15	10	13	45	53	55	UEFA Cup
10. West Ham Utd	38	13	10	15	42	50	49	
11. Tottenham	38	11	13	14	66	61	46	UEFA Cup
12. Newcastle United	38	11	10	17	45	65	43	
13. Middlesbrough	38	10	12	16	43	53	42	
14. Wigan Athletic	38	10	10	18	34	51	40	
15. Sunderland	38	11	6	21	36	59	39	
16. Bolton Wanderers	38	9	10	19	36	54	37	
17. Fulham	38	8	12	18	38	60	36	
18. Reading	38	10	6	22	41	66	36	Relegated
19. Birmingham City	38	8	11	19	46	62	35	Relegated
20. Derby County	38	1	8	29	20	89	11	Relegated

Can you spot the ball?

Answers on page 60/61

Quiz Answers

CITY OF MANCHESTER STADIUM QUIZ
(From page 16&17)

1. It was the ball used for the 2008 UEFA Cup Final

2. Ricky Hatton's 'Homecoming fight' v Juan Lazcano

3. State-of-the-art scoreboards

4. At the corner of the pitch, of course!

5. Zola was taking part in the England v the Rest of the World for the PFA Centenary match

6. The manager's dug-out by the side of the pitch

7. It's Richard Dunnes' armband in the home dressing room

8. One of the four domes situated around the stadium allowing access to the upper seating levels

SPOT THE BALL A (From page 43)

Answer B4

SPOT THE BALL B (From page 43)

Answer E1

THE BIG CITY QUIZ
(From page 28&29)

01 – Elano (1pt)
02 – Sheffield United & Derby (3pts)
03 – Chelsea & Liverpool (1pt)
04 – Four – Dunne (twice), Petrov and Ireland (3pts)
05 – West Ham (1pt)
06 – Manchester United (3pts)
07 – Spurs (1pt)
08 – West Ham (3pts)
09 – Elano (1pt)
10 – Slovakia (3pts)
11 – False – it was Liverpool (1pt)
12 – Les Chapman (3pts)
13 – Chelsea (1pt)
14 – Aggregate: 4-2 (3pts)
15 – Valencia (1pt)
16 – Norwich City (3pts)
17 – Heerenveen (1pt)
18 – Wales (3pts)
19 – Three (1pt)
20 – 14 (3pts)
21 – Valeri Bojinov (1pt)
22 – Vidic (3pts)
23 – Geovanni – 1 minute (1pt)
24 – Javier Garrido (3pts)
25 – Rolando Bianchi (1pt)
26 – 98 (3pts)
27 – Michael Johnson (1pt)
28 – 6th place (3pts)
29 – Micah Richards (1pt)
30 – Manchester United, Newcastle United & Sunderland (3pts)
31 – Elano & Petrov (1pt)
32 – 10 (3pts)
33 – Sam Williamson (1pt)
34 – 2-0 (3pts)
35 – Nedum Onuoha (1pt)
36 – Ched Evans (3pts)
37 – Crystal palace & Blackpool (1pt)
38 – Bolton Wanderers 4-2 (3pts)

WHO IS CELEBRATING QUIZ?
(From page 30)

1. Benjani v Fulham
2. Martin Petrov v Portsmouth
3. Darius Vassell v Sunderland
4. Elano v Sunderland
5. Nedum Onuoha v Spurs
6. Danny Sturridge v Sheffield United
7. Elano v West Ham (FA Cup R)
8. Elano v Newcastle (H)

SPOT THE BALL A (From page 58)

A B C D E F

1 2 3 4

Answer B4

SPOT THE BALL B (From page 58)

A B C D E F

1 2 3 4

Answer B2/C2

GUESS WHO (From page 53)

A) JOE HART ≪

B) MICAH RICHARDS ≫

C) VEDRAN ≪ CORLUKA

D) MARTIN PETROV ≫

CROSSWORD (From page 31)
– How did you do?

WORD SEARCH (From page 23)
Did you solve wordsearch mystery? Here are the answers

digibet
le coq sportif
le coq sportif
Thomas C
Thomas
Cook.com
Lucozade SPORT
Lucozade SPORT
Thom